CW01512584

ONOMATOPE

The Fantastic World of
Japanese Symbolic Words

Supervisor
ONO Masahiro

ナツメ社

Supervisor ONO Masahiro

Born in Iwate prefecture in 1958, Ono is a professor at Meiji University, School of
Arts and Letters who specializes in the historical investigation of Japanese language
(literature, vocabulary and semantics). He serves as vice president of the Society for
Japanese Linguistics and a president of the Modern Japanese Language Research
Association, and has written numerous books on Japanese language and onomatope.

Book Design	NAITO Yuji
Illustration	OKAMURA Ryota
English Author	ONODERA Shuku
English Checker	HISAMATSU Noriko
English Proofreader	Freya Martin
Associate Editor	YOSHIHARA Tomoe (Three Season Co., Ltd.)
Editor	KODAKA Mari (Natsume Shuppan Kikaku Co., Ltd.)

ONOMATOPE
The Fantastic World of Japanese Symbolic Words
First Edition November 2019

Publisher
Natsumesha Co.,Ltd.
Natsume Bldg. 1F 1-52 Kanda-JImbocho, Chiyoda-ku,Tokyo,
Japan 101-0051

Production
Natsume Shuppan Kikaku Co., Ltd.

Printing
Lan Printing Co., Ltd.

The onomatope is a generic term of echoic words (transcription of animal cries and sounds into human voice) and mimic words (sound expression of the appearance, emotion or senses of human beings or things). Japanese people are familiar with onomatopoeic words and use them in daily life. One of their appeals is the expressive preciseness that ordinally words do not have, so the exact paraphrasing of onomatopoeic words can be a challenge.

This book tries to explain the meanings and nuances of Japanese onomatopoeic words as plainly as possible with illustrations. I hope you will take it easy and explore the fascinating world of the onomatope.

Supervisor
ONO Masahiro

「オノマトペ」とは、動物の鳴き声や物音を人間の音声に写し換えた「擬音語」と、人間や物事の様子、感情や感覚を、言葉の音がもつ感性で表現した「擬態語」の総称です。

日本人には、とても身近な言葉で、誰しもが日常で使っています。その魅力のひとつは、普通の言葉だけでは言い表せないことを、ずばり言い表せる表現力にありますので、「オノマトペ」を別の言葉で、すみずみまで正確に言い換えるのは、じつはとても難しいことです。

この本では、その意味やニュアンスを、できるだけわかりやすく伝えられるようイラスト付きで紹介しました。気持ちを楽にもって、この魅力的な「オノマトペ」の世界を感じとっていただけたらうれしいです。

監修　小野正弘

CONTENTS

目次

PART 1 人の表情や気持ちを表す
EXPRESSIONS & FEELINGS
>>> 007

PART 2 人の動きを表す
BODY MOVEMENTS
>>> 021

PART 3 人の心や体の状態を表す
MENTAL & PHYSICAL CONDITIONS
>>> 041

PART 4 性格や体型のいろいろ
PERSONALITIES & BODY SHAPES
>>> 069

PART 5 物や人の動きを表す
MOVEMENTS OF OBJECTS & PEOPLE
>>> 081

PART 6 物の状態を表す
STATE OF THINGS
>>> 097

PART 7 物事の程度や様子を表す
DEGREES & MANNERS
>>> 123

PART 8 温度や天気のいろいろ
TEMPERATURES & WEATHER
>>> 145

PART 9 食事や料理に使う表現
FOOD & CUISINE
>>> 157

PART 10 音のいろいろ
SOUNDS
>>> 179

INDEX 索引
>>> 201

COMPOSITION OF THE BOOK

本の構成

This book features 201 onomatopes that are categorized into 10 themes. Each page has an onomatope with its core meaning, sample sentence and illustration. Supplementary remarks like synonyms or points to notes are at the foot of the page.

パート・タイトル
Part / Title

オノマトペ
Onomatopoeia

読み方
Pronunciation

トラックナンバー
Track number

基本的な意味
Basic meanning

例文
Example

類語・ポイント・注などの補足事項
Synonym / Point / Note etc.

分類
Classification

Sample page

PART 1　人の表情や気持ちを表す

🎧 001 **ニコニコ**
[nikoniko]

穏やかで温かい笑みを浮かべ続ける様子
a long, warm and gentle smile

Example
あの人はいつもニコニコして感じがいい。
That lady is always beaming and nice.

Synonym
ニッコリ [nikkori] Nikoniko is a lasting smile, while nikkori is a momentary smile.

008　▶ LAUGH

BONUS 　購入者特典

音声ダウンロードができます！

Downloadable audio files available

ナツメ社のホームページ『ONOMATOPE　The Fantastic World of Japanese Symbolic Words』のページより音声ダウンロードが可能です。
Audio files are available on the website of Natsumesha:
ONOMATOPE The Fantastic World of Japanese Symbolic Words.

※ 日本語のイントネーションについて … 見出しのオノマトペの発音と、例文のオノマトペの発音は、そのオノマトペのあとに続く言葉の影響によって、イントネーションが変わることがあります。
※ The intonation of onomatope may change according to the words that follow it.

MAIN CHARACTERS

この本にでてくる主な登場人物

♥えり・Eri
主人公 21歳

大学3年生。東京の大学の外国語学部に通う。明るくて元気な性格。

Leading Character · 21 years old
A third-year college student in the faculty of foreign studies at a college in Tokyo. Crisp and cheery.

♥まな・Mana
えりの姉・25歳

中学校の英語の先生。授業では厳しいが生徒から人気がある。しっかり者。

Eri's sister · 25 years old
An English teacher at a junior high school. Strict at class but popular among students. Mature.

♠けんた・Kenta
えりの弟・17歳

高校2年生。サッカー部に所属。少しおっちょこちょいだけど頑張り屋さん。

Eri's brother · 17 years old
A second-year high school student. A member of the school soccer club. A bit scatterbrained but hardworking.

♥なおみ・Naomi
えりの親友・21歳

えりと同じ大学に通う。国際交流サークルに所属。やさしい性格。

Eri's friend · 21 years old
A student at the same college as Eri's. A member of an international exchange club. Gentle.

♠マックス・Max
えりの家の愛犬・3歳

近所の人気者。いざというときは頼れる番犬。食べることと寝ることが好き。

Eri's dog · three years old
Popular among neighbors. A reliable guard dog in a time of emergency. Likes eating and sleeping.

♠ジェームズ・James
まなのボーイフレンド・27歳

まなと同じ中学校の英語の先生。ロサンゼルス生まれ。日本が大好き。

Mana's boy friend · 27 years old
An English teacher at the same junior high school as Mana's. Born in Los Angeles. Japanophilia.

♠じょうじ・Joji
えりたちのパパ・50歳

会社員。仕事熱心で真面目な性格。旅行とドライブが大好き。

Eri's dad · 50 years old
A company employee. Hardworking and serious. A travel and driving lover.

♥まり・Mari
えりたちのママ・48歳

主婦。料理が得意。読書と映画鑑賞が趣味。やさしい性格。ちょっと心配性。

Eri's mother · 48 years old
Housewife. Good at cooking. A book and movie lover. Gentle and a bit worrier.

人の表情や
気持ちを表す

EXPRESSIONS
& FEELINGS

🎧001 ニコニコ

[nikoniko]

おだやかで温かい笑みを浮かべ続ける様子
a long, warm and gentle smile

Example

あの人はいつも**ニコニコ**していて感じがいい。
That lady is always beaming and nice.

Synonym

ニッコリ [nikkori] *Nikoniko* is a lasting smile, while *nikkori* is a momentary smile.

🎧002 ゲラゲラ
[geragera]

大声で心の底から笑う様子や、その声
a deep, loud, hearty laugh, especially a laughing voice

Example

芸人さんのトークがおもしろすぎて、みんなでゲラゲラと笑った。
All of us guffawed because the comedian's story was so hilarious.

Point ··

  A slightly coarse laugh.

🎧003 ニヤニヤ
[niyaniya]

意味ありげにうす笑いを浮かべる様子
a thin, expressive smile

叱られたのにニヤニヤしているなんて、失礼だ！
You are grinning when you are being scolded! How rude!

Point ···

A silent laugh when you recall or think of something.

∩004 クスクス

[kusukusu]

ひそやかに笑う様子や、その声

a quiet laugh, especially the voice

Example

練習中にズボンがやぶれてクスクス笑われてしまった。

Everyone snickered at me as my pants got ripped during practice.

🎧005 しくしく
[shikushiku]

勢いなく弱々しく泣く様子や、その声

a feeble cry, especially a crying voice

Example

悲しいことがあったのか、部屋でしくしく泣いている。

He is weeping perhaps because something sad happened to him.

Note ···

We also say *shikushiku* when we feel a dull, cramping pain.

∩006 エーン

[een]

幼い子どもなどが、心の底から大声を上げて泣く様子
a deep, loud, hearty cry like a little child

Example

迷子の子どもが、お母さんを求めてエーンと泣いている。
The lost child is boohooing, looking for her mom.

Synonym ··
エンエン [en'en]

🎧007 わんわん

[wanwan]

まわりを気にせず、大きな声をあげて泣く様子や、その声
an unselfconscious loud cry, especially a crying voice

Example

この映画のラストシーンは、いつ観てもわんわん泣いてしまう。
The last scene of this movie always makes me bawl.

Synonym ···

わーん [waan]

Note ···

Wanwan also means bowwow (see p. 196).

🎧008 プンプン
[punpun]

ひどく腹を立てて機嫌の悪い様子
very angry; displeased

Example

デートに遅刻してしまって、彼女にプンプンされた。
I was late for the date and my girlfriend got pissed off.

Note ··

Punpun also means a strong odor.

🎧009 ムカムカ

[mukamuka]

怒りが心の底からこみあげてくる様子

deep rage

Example

ひどい悪口を言われて、思い出すだけでムカムカする。

I was really trash-talked and just thinking about it made me queasy.

Note ··

Mukamuka also means a heavy, uncomfortable stomach.

⌒010 カンカン
[kankan]

すぐには許してくれそうもないほどはげしく怒る様子
unforgiving rage

Example

重要なことを伝え忘れ、上司がカンカンに怒ってしまった。
I forgot to tell my boss something important and he got mad at me.

Note ⋯⋯⋯⋯⋯⋯⋯⋯⋯⋯⋯⋯⋯⋯⋯⋯⋯⋯⋯⋯⋯⋯⋯⋯⋯⋯⋯⋯⋯⋯⋯⋯
Kankan can also mean (1) metallic clangs or (2) burning charcoal.

🎧011 ウキウキ

[ukiuki]

心のはずむ様子／晴れやかな様子
exhilarated and brightened up

Example

今日の夕飯は、大好きなハンバーグだと聞いて**ウキウキ**した。
I felt happy when I heard we were having hamburger steak for today's dinner, which is my favorite.

🎧012 ほくほく
[hokuhoku]

満足しきって、うれしさを隠しきれない様子
fully satisfied and can't hide your joy

Example

お小遣いがいつもより多くもらえて ほくほく した気分になる。
I'm really pleased as I got more allowance than usual.

Note
Hokuhoku is also used to describe a food texture (see p. 178).

Happy scenes

🎧013 ランラン
[ranran]

気分が浮き立って楽しそうな様子

light-hearted and happy-looking

Example

お菓子をもらった子どもが
ランランとスキップをしている。

The kid got sweets and is skipping around with gusto.

Note

Ranran also means glaring eyes.

🎧014 ルンルン
[runrun]

気分が解放されて浮き立ち、
自然に鼻歌も出そうな様子

such unbound enthusiasm and so cheered up that you automatically start humming

Example

久しぶりのデートで、
ルンルンと心がはずんだ。

I was super excited for my first date in a while.

人の動きを表す

BODY MOVEMENTS

🎧015 スタスタ

[sutasuta]

速いスピードで、わき目も振らず歩いていく様子
walking straight ahead quickly

スタスタ歩いていたらすぐに駅が見えた。
I walked on briskly and soon found the station.

🎧016 ウロウロ
[urouro]

どうしたらよいかわからないまま、あたりを動き回る様子
moving around without knowing what to do

Example

建物の入口が分からずウロウロしてしまった。
I wandered around until I found the entrance to the building.

🎧017 てくてく
[tekuteku]

同じ調子でひたすら歩き続ける様子
keeping walking at a constant pace

Example

バスがなくなり、てくてくと家まで夜道を歩いた。
I missed the last bus and hoofed it home at night.

🎧018 ぴょんぴょん

[pyonpyon]

何度もはずみをつけてとび上がる様子
jumping vigorously and repeatedly

Example

子どもが楽しそうに縄跳びをぴょんぴょんととんでいる。
Children are happily jumping rope up and down.

Synonym ⋯⋯

ぴょん [pyon] *Pyonpyon* describes repetitive jumps, while *pyon* means a single jump.

🎧019 ペラペラ

[perapera]

外国語などをよどみなく話す様子
speaking a foreign language etc. fluently

Example

彼女は留学生活が長く、英語がペラペラだ。
She has long studied abroad and speaks English fluently.

Note ··
Perapera is also an expression to describe something thin like paper.

🎧020 ぶつぶつ

[butsubutsu]

よく聞き取れないほどの大きさで言葉を発する様子

uttering words in a barely audible voice

Example

何を考えているのか、一人でぶつぶつ言っている。

He is mumbling to himself. I wonder what he's thinking about.

Note ··

Butsubutsu also means (1) dissatisfaction or (2) small boils on skin.

🎧021 ハキハキ

[hakihaki]

態度や物言いが賢く、手早く、よどみがない様子

clever, quick and smooth in speech and action

Example

お客様からの質問には、ハキハキと答えることが大切だ。

The important thing is to answer questions from your customers clearly and briskly.

🎧022 ひそひそ

[hisohiso]

人に聞かれないように隠れて話す様子や、その声
talking in secret so that nobody can hear you

Example

こっちを時折見ながらひそひそ話をしていて感じ悪い。
They are disgusting because they are looking at me and whispering.

🎧023 ちらちら

[chirachira]

ちらちら

人や物を断続的に見る様子／物が見え隠れする様子

looking at something or someone again and again; something appearing and disappearing

Example

テレビに出ている有名人が近くにいたのでちらちら見てしまった。

I saw a TV celebrity up close, so I couldn't stop glancing at him.

Synonym ....

ちらり [chirari] *Chirachira* is repeated glances, while *chirari* is a single glance.

🎧024 ジロジロ

[jirojiro]

相手への遠慮がなく、強い視線でしつこく見つめる様子
staring at someone strongly and unreservedly

Example

派手な服装で出かけたら、みんなにジロジロと見られた。
I went out in showy clothes and everyone stared at me.

Synonym ···

ジロリ **[jirori]** *Jirori* means a stronger gaze than *jirojiro*, or a glare.

🎧025 テキパキ

［tekipaki］

物事がすばやく的確な対応で進む様子／動作が機敏な様子

things moving on quickly and appropriately; acting agilely

Example

テキパキと仕事をこなしたあとは
おいしいディナーを食べに行く予定だ。

I'll get the job done quickly and then go out to eat a delicious dinner.

∩026 サクサク

[sakusaku]

物事が滞りなく進む様子

things moving on smoothly

Example

みんなからよいアイデアがでたので、
打ち合わせはサクサクと進んだ。

Everyone voiced their ideas so we quickly moved forward
with the meeting.

Note ....

Sakusaku is also used (1) to describe how people don't mince their words or
(2) to express a food texture (See p. 174).

∩027 がやがや

[gayagaya]

多くの人々が騒々しい声で話す様子

many people speaking loudly

Example

周りががやがやしていたので、話がよく聞きとれなかった。

Everybody was chattering away and I couldn't hear what she was saying.

🎧028 チョキチョキ

［chokichoki］

はさみを軽快に動かしたり、
物を切り刻んだりする様子や、その音
moving scissors dexterously; snipping something; snipping sound

Example

職人さんが大きな布を手際よく チョキチョキ 切った。
The craftsman deftly cut a big piece of cloth with scissors.

Trivia ⋯⋯⋯⋯⋯⋯⋯⋯⋯⋯⋯⋯⋯⋯⋯⋯⋯⋯⋯⋯⋯⋯⋯⋯⋯⋯⋯⋯⋯⋯⋯⋯⋯⋯⋯⋯⋯
Choki means scissors in the rock-paper-scissors game.

🎧029 ぶるぶる

[buruburu]

体全体がはげしくふるえる様子や、その音

the whole body trembling violently; trembling sound

Example

昨晩から北風が強く、朝のあまりの寒さにぶるぶると震えた。

A strong, north wind has been blowing all night. It was so cold that my body was still trembling violently this morning.

Note ··

Buruburu also describes how you tremble with fear.

🎧030 ガクガク

[gakugaku]

物がゆるんで動きやすくなっている様子／ひどくふるえ続ける様子

something getting loose and unstable; something shaking hard

Example

はじめてのフルマラソンに挑戦したら、途中で足がガクガクになった。

I tried to run a whole marathon for the first time and my legs gave out along the way.

🎧031 ガバッと

[gabatto]

瞬間的に大きな動作をはげしく行う様子

making a big movement instantaneously

Example

けたたましい目覚ましの音で慌ててガバッと起きた。

The alarm clock rang really loud and I sprung up in bed.

🎧032 ぐっすり

[gussuri]

何者にもさまたげられることなく深く眠る様子
sleeping deeply without any interruption

Example

昨日はたくさん体を動かしたので、ぐっすり眠れた。
I was very active all day, so I had a good sleep.

Sleepy scenes

🎧033 ウトウト

[utouto]

眠気をもよおす様子／
眠りの浅い様子

feeling sleepy;
snoozing

Example

穏やかな春の日射しで、
ついウトウトとしてしまった。

I drifted off to sleep in the soft
spring sunlight.

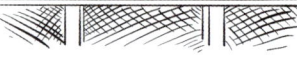

🎧034 グーグー

[guuguu]

大きないびきの音／
爆睡※する様子　※俗語

a big snoring sound;
sleeping like a log

Example

グーグーと周りを気にせず寝ている。

He is openly snoring in his sleep.

Note

The Japanese word 爆睡 (bakusui) is slang
(not a standard written word but a daily
spoken word, dialect or vulgar word)

人の心や体の状態を表す

MENTAL & PHYSICAL CONDITIONS

🎧035 アタフタ
[atafuta]

混乱してひどくあわてる様子
confused and panicked

Example

急にお客さんがやってきてアタフタしてしまった。
A guest suddenly arrived and we made a great fuss.

🎧036 せかせか
[sekaseka]

余裕がなく、動作などの落ち着かない様子
too busy and restless

Example

母はいつもスーパーの中をせかせかと歩きまわっている。
My mother is always walking around the supermarket restlessly.

🎧037 オロオロ

[orooro]

どうしていいかわからず落ち着きを失っている様子

at your wit's end and impatient

Example

突然予想していなかった質問をされて、オロオロした。

I got flustered when someone asked me an unexpected question.

⌾038 ジタバタ

[jitabata]

あわてもがく様子／あせってむだな努力をする様子
flustered; rush and make a useless effort

`Example`

弟はいつもテストの前日になってからジタバタしている。
My brother always starts to make vain efforts on the day before the test.

Note ···

Jitabata is also used to describe how you move your limbs and body desperately.

🎧039 ソワソワ
[sowasowa]

気持ちや動作の落ち着かない様子／
気がかりなことや、期待で浮きあし立つ様子

twitchy feeling/action: agitated with anxiety/expectation

Example

娘は明日バレエの発表会なのでソワソワしている。

My daughter is twitchy about tomorrow's ballet recital.

🎧040 ハラハラ

[harahara]

気をもんで危うさを感じている様子
feeling worried and endangered

この恋愛小説はハラハラする展開が続く。
This love story is full of thrilling developments.

Note ···

Harahara also describes how thin objects like leaves fall apart.

🎧041 ワクワク

[wakuwaku]

喜びや期待で胸がおどる様子

excited with joy or expectation

Example

夏休みの海外旅行が楽しみで今からワクワクしている。

We are thrilled about our trip overseas during our summer vacation.

🎧042 ドキドキ

[dokidoki]

気持ちの高ぶりやはげしい運動でこどうが早くなる様子
heart-quickening due to excitement or a heavy workout

Example

好きな子に告白するチャンスが突然おとずれてドキドキした。

My heart pounded when I suddenly had a chance to ask my crush for a date.

Synonym ....

ドキン [dokin] exited and your heart beats strongly

🎧043 ジーン

[jiin]

感動に包み込まれる様子

deeply moved

Example

胸を打つドラマの展開に思わず ジーン とする。

I was really touched by the drama because it was so moving.

Note ···

Jiin is also used to describe (1) body numbness or (2) anesthesia due to heat or cold.

🎧044 ホロリ

[horori]

同情して心が動いたり、もの悲しい気持ちになったりする様子
empathetic/melancholic

Example

動物の親子のドキュメントを見てホロリとした。

I was almost moved to tears when I saw a documentary film about animal parents and their children.

Note ⋯⋯⋯⋯⋯⋯⋯⋯⋯⋯⋯⋯⋯⋯⋯⋯⋯⋯⋯⋯⋯⋯⋯⋯⋯⋯⋯⋯⋯⋯

Horori also means a single tear falling down your face.

🎧045 ビクッと

[bikutto]

驚きおそれて、反射的に身をふるわせたりこわばらせたりする様子

physically shaking; stiffened as an automatic reaction to surprise/fear

Example

突然大きな声を出されて、ビクッとしてしまった。

I was startled when someone suddenly shouted.

Trivia ⋯⋯⋯⋯⋯⋯⋯⋯⋯⋯⋯⋯⋯⋯⋯⋯⋯⋯⋯⋯⋯⋯⋯⋯⋯⋯⋯⋯⋯⋯⋯

Bikkuri is often used to express surprise.

⌒046 ギクッと

[gikutto]

一瞬強く驚きおそれて心に衝撃がはしる様子

extremely surprised, scared and shocked briefly

Example

考えていたことを言い当てられて、ギクッとした。

I was shocked when she correctly guessed what I was thinking about.

Note ⋯⋯⋯⋯⋯⋯⋯⋯⋯⋯⋯⋯⋯⋯⋯⋯⋯⋯⋯⋯⋯⋯⋯⋯⋯⋯⋯⋯⋯⋯⋯

Gikutto is also used when your lower back hurts.

🎧047 がっかり

[gakkari]

落胆・失望した様子

depressed; disappointed

Example

期待していたプレゼントをもらえなくて**がっかり**した。

I was disappointed because I didn't get the present I was supposed to get.

Point ....

You say *gakkari* when the result is not what you expected.

🎧048 ガーン

[gaan]

心理的に強い衝撃を受ける様子
receiving a strong emotional shock

Example

ガーン、ソースをお気に入りの服に落としてしまった。
Bummer! I dropped sauce on my favorite clothes.

Point ⋯⋯⋯⋯⋯⋯⋯⋯⋯⋯⋯⋯⋯⋯⋯⋯⋯⋯⋯⋯⋯⋯⋯⋯⋯⋯⋯⋯⋯⋯⋯⋯⋯⋯⋯⋯⋯⋯⋯
Gaan is used when you get a great shock.

🎧049 ペコペコ

[pekopeko]

ひどくお腹がすいた様子

feeling very hungry

Example

朝からずっと食べていないので、おなかがペコペコだ。

I'm starving because I haven't eaten anything since morning.

Note ⋯⋯⋯⋯⋯⋯⋯⋯⋯⋯⋯⋯⋯⋯⋯⋯⋯⋯⋯⋯⋯⋯⋯⋯⋯⋯⋯⋯⋯⋯⋯⋯⋯⋯⋯⋯

Pekopeko also describes (1) repeated bows or (2) thin, elastic boards repeatedly dented or bent.

⌂050 カラカラ

[karakara]

乾ききっている様子

extremely dry

Example

たくさん走ったので、のどがカラカラになった。

I've run a lot, so I'm parched now.

Note ···

Karakara also describes a clear sound produced when metal or wooden objects hit each other.

🎧051 うじうじ

[ujiuji]

しなければならないと知りつつためらっている様子

feeling hesitant when you know you should do something

Example

言いたいことがあるのに口に出さず、うじうじしている。

He is moping around and is not saying what he really wants to say.

🎧052 もじもじ

[mojimoji]

遠慮したり、恥ずかしがったり、
決心がつかなかったりして気をもむ様子

squirming, feeling hesitant, shy, or of two minds

Example

好きな人の前で顔を真っ赤にして、もじもじしている。

She is blushing in front of her crush and fidgeting.

🎧053 うっとり
[uttori]

美しいもの、好ましいものなどによる快感に身をゆだねている様子
enjoying something beautiful or favorable

Example

思わず うっとり するようなキレイな音色が聞こえてきた。
I can hear a beautiful sound. That's enchanting.

Point ....
Uttori describes how you are fascinated and enchanted by something.

🎧054 **キュン**

[kyun]

なにかを発見した感動で、胸がときめく様子
heart-fluttering with some new discovery

Example

年上の友人が見せたかわいい笑顔が意外で、胸が**キュン**とした。
My guy friend had a surprisingly cute smile so my heart skipped a beat.

Point ···

Kyun means exciting feelings when you see something cute or are falling in love.

🎧055 ウンザリ

[unzari]

長すぎたり、くどかったりしていやになる様子
feeling tired of something too lengthy or long-winded

Example

同じ話を何度も聞いて、ウンザリしている。
I'm sick of hearing the same story again and again.

🎧056 ダラダラ

[daradara]

物事がしまりなく長引く様子

sloppy and prolonged

Example

今日は休みだったので、家の中でダラダラして過ごした。

I had a day off today so I just lazed around in my house.

Note

Daradara also describes how a lot of sweat keeps running down your face or body.

🎧057 ヘトヘト

[hetoheto]

疲れきって、体にほとんど力がなくなってしまう様子

exhausted and almost drained of energy

Example

部活の強化練習では、ヘトヘトになるまで、思い切り走り続けた。

We kept running hard until we got exhausted at the training camp of our club.

🎧058 ぐったり

[guttari]

これ以上ないほど疲労して力がぬけた様子
couldn't be more exhausted and weak

Example

１日中忙しく働いて、ぐったりしている。
I'm totally listless after working hard all day.

🎧059 ムズムズ

[muzumuzu]

虫がはいまわるような感触を肌や心でうける様子
feel uncomfortable physically or mentally

Example

花粉症なので、春は鼻が ムズムズ する。
My nose itches in spring because I have hayfever.

Note ⋯⋯⋯⋯⋯⋯⋯⋯⋯⋯⋯⋯⋯⋯⋯⋯⋯⋯⋯⋯⋯⋯⋯⋯⋯⋯⋯⋯⋯⋯⋯
Muzumuzu is also used to describe how you are dying to do something.

🎧060 チクチク

[chikuchiku]

先のとがったもので小刻みにくり返し刺す様子や、
その刺激によるかゆみや痛み

repeatedly sticking something with a pointed end little by little; itching and pain from such stimuli

Example

このセーターは、毛糸がチクチクする。

This wool sweater is making me itch.

Note ⋯⋯⋯⋯⋯⋯⋯⋯⋯⋯⋯⋯⋯⋯⋯⋯⋯⋯⋯⋯⋯⋯⋯⋯⋯⋯⋯⋯⋯⋯⋯⋯⋯⋯⋯⋯⋯⋯

Chikuchiku is also used to (1) make wisecracks or (2) sew with a needle.

Painful scenes

🎧061 ズキズキ
[zukizuki]

絶え間なく、
重くひびくように痛む様子

**feeling dull, rebounding pain
continuously**

Example

ズキズキとひどい頭痛がする。

**I have a throbbing
headache.**

Synonym ···

ズキン [zukin] momentary strong pain

🎧062 ジンジン
[jinjin]

絶え間なく、
痺れるように痛む様子

**feeling continuous,
tingling pain**

Example

机の脚にぶつけたスネが
ジンジンする。

**I hit my shin against
the table leg and it tingles.**

性格や体型の いろいろ

PERSONALITIES &
BODY SHAPES

🎧063 サッパリ

[sappari]

性格、態度などがくどくなく、すがすがしく清潔感のある様子

frank character/attitude, with freshness and cleanliness

Example

小さなことは気にせず、サッパリとしていると周りから言われる。

Everyone says I am straightforward and don't worry about details.

Note ⋯⋯⋯⋯⋯⋯⋯⋯⋯⋯⋯⋯⋯⋯⋯⋯⋯⋯⋯⋯⋯⋯⋯⋯⋯⋯⋯⋯⋯⋯⋯⋯⋯⋯

Sappari is also used to describe (1) how you feel good and refreshed or (2) how something tastes non-fatty and refreshing.

⌖064 キッチリ

[kicchiri]

よく整っていたり、正確な様子

tidy or precise

Example

姉はキッチリとした性格で、前日までに準備をすませるほうだ。

My sister is a neat person and gets everything ready the day before.

♫065 おっとり

[ottori]

人柄、態度などが間延びしていると思えるほど落ちついている様子
calm, almost sluggish character/attitude

Example

彼女はいつも**おっとり**構えて、人とはあまり争わない。
She is always placid and seldom confronts others.

🎧066 サバサバ

[sabasaba]

動作や性格などにこだわりがない様子
not picky about what you do or think

彼はサバサバとした性格で、根にもつことがない。
He is not two-faced and is good at forgetting things.

🎧067 ちゃっかり

[chakkari]

抜け目がないのだが、どこかにくめない様子
shrewd but somewhat lovable

Example

弟はちゃっかりとおみやげを2つもらってきた。
My brother shrewdly got two gifts.

∩068 ハッキリ

[hakkiri]

明確で、迷いや遠慮がない様子

definite, without hesitation or ambivalence

彼は必ずハッキリと、自分の意見を言う。

He never minces his words when he voices his opinion.

Synonym ···

ハキハキ **[hakihaki]** speaking clearly and briskly

🎧069 ガリガリ

[garigari]

骨や血管が浮き出るくらいひどく痩せている様子

so skinny that bones and veins are visible

Example

クラスメートがダイエットのしすぎでガリガリにやせて心配だ。

I'm worried about my classmate who is following an excessive diet and getting bony.

Note ....

Garigari also describes how you keep nibbling at something hard.

🎧070 ヒョロヒョロ
[hyorohyoro]

背は高いが痩せてひよわな様子。細長く弱々しげにのびている様子
tall but thin and weak; slender and fragile

Example

兄は、ヒョロヒョロとしていて頼りない。
My brother is gangly and spineless.

🎧071 ガッシリ

[gasshiri]

体・構造などが強くたくましい様子
strong, tough constitution/structure

Example

彼はガッシリとしていて、かなりトレーニングしているようだ。
He is well-built. Looks like he is working out a lot.

∩072 ぽっちゃり
[pocchari]

まるく肥えてかわいらしい様子
plump and cute

Example

近所のネコは、ぽっちゃりしていてかわいい。
Our neighbor's cat is plump and cute.

Overweight scenes

🎧073 プクプク
[pukupuku]

かわいらしく、
やわらかくふくらんだ様子
cute, soft and puffy

Example

赤ちゃんの手足は**プクプク**していて、
思わず指で押してみたくなる。
A baby's limbs are so chubby that I feel like pushing them with my fingers.

Note ....
Pukupuku also describes water bubbles.

🎧074 ムチムチ
[muchimuchi]

肉付きがよく張りのある様子
well fleshed and resilient

Example

年末年始で、
ごちそうをたくさん食べたら
ムチムチした体型になった。
I ate sumptuous meals during the New Year holidays and became pudgy.

物や人の
動きを表す

MOVEMENTS OF OBJECTS
& PEOPLE

🎧075 ユラユラ

[yurayura]

無抵抗に何度もゆれ動く様子

swaying repeatedly without resistance

Example

耳元でユラユラゆれるイヤリングがかわいい。

Her swinging earrings are cute.

🎧076 グラグラ

[guragura]

固定せず不安定な様子
not fixed and also unstable

Example

椅子の足が グラグラ して、落ち着かない。
The chair legs are rickety and unstable.

Note ⋯⋯⋯⋯⋯⋯⋯⋯⋯⋯⋯⋯⋯⋯⋯⋯⋯⋯⋯⋯⋯⋯⋯⋯⋯⋯⋯

Guragura also means severe dizziness.

🎧077 **フラフラ**

[furafura]

安定感がなく、力なくゆれ動く様子
unstable and swaying helplessly

Example

頭が**フラフラ**するのは、昨夜の徹夜の疲れがたまっているせいだ。
I feel dizzy because I'm exhausted after no sleep last night.

Note ⋯⋯⋯⋯⋯⋯⋯⋯⋯⋯⋯⋯⋯⋯⋯⋯⋯⋯⋯⋯⋯⋯⋯⋯⋯⋯⋯⋯⋯⋯⋯⋯⋯⋯
Furafura is also used to describe shivering due to fear or cold.

🎧078 ガタガタ

[gatagata]

固いものが、ゆれたり触れ合ったりして発する重く騒々しい音

heavy, loud noise made when solid objects swing or touch each other

Example

古い家なので、強い風がふくとガタガタと窓がゆれる。

This is an old house and the window rattles when the wind blows hard.

Synonym ···

カタカタ [katakata] smaller sound than gatagata

Note ···

Gatagata also describes something not going well, such as a failed presentation or a disassembled organization.

🎧079 ひらひら
[hirahira]

薄く軽いものが空中でゆれ動く様子
thin, light object swaying in the air

Example

ひらひらと舞い落ちる桜の花びらがキレイだ。
The fluttery cherry blossom petals are beautiful.

Note ···

Hirahira also describes something lightly flaunting.

🎧080 ポチャン

[pochan]

小さなものが水中に落ちる音
sound made when a small object falls into water

Example

カエルが池にポチャンという音を立てて飛び込んだ。
A frog plopped into the pond.

🎧081 ドサッと

[dosatto]

重いものがわずかな間に落ちたり倒れたりする音

sound made when a heavy object falls or comes down all of a sudden

Example

屋根から雪が ドサッと 落ちてきた。

Snow thumped down from the roof.

🎧082 パラパラ

[parapara]

本などのページが軽く次々にめくられる音

sound of the pages of a book etc. flipping lightly

パラパラと雑誌をめくっていたら、とある記事にふと目が留まった。

Flicking through a magazine, an article caught my eye.

Note ⋯⋯⋯⋯⋯⋯⋯⋯⋯⋯⋯⋯⋯⋯⋯⋯⋯⋯⋯⋯⋯⋯⋯⋯⋯⋯⋯⋯⋯⋯⋯⋯⋯⋯⋯

Parapara also describes the sound made when light objects like raindrops or leaves are falling.

🎧083 ポキン

[pokin]

細くてかたいもの、細く続いているものが
突然折れる様子や、その音

a thin, hard object or a slender object breaking suddenly;
especially the sound

Example

強風にあおられて枝がポキンと音を立てて折れた。

The tree was hit by a gust of wind and the branch broke
with a snap.

🎧084 バキッと

[bakitto]

太くて丈夫なものが折れる様子や、その音

a thick, sturdy object breaking; especially the sound

Example

三振して思わずバットを叩きつけたら、バキッという音がして折れた。

I got struck out and slammed my bat, which cracked with a snap.

Synonym ....

バキッと [pakitto] describes a smaller and higher sound than bakitto.

🎧085 プカプカ

[pukapuka]

軽快に水に浮く様子や、浮いて流れる様子
floating on water lightly, or floating down

Example

浮き輪に乗って海で**プカプカ**浮かんでいるとリラックスできる。
Floating lightly on an inner tube in the sea is relaxing.

Note ···

Pukapuka also means big tobacco puffs.

🎧086 コロコロ

[korokoro]

丸いものや小さなものが転がっていくときの様子や、その音
a round or small object rolling; especially the sound

Example

コロコロと転がるボールを犬が楽しそうに追いかけている。
A dog is pleasantly chasing a rolling ball.

Note ··

Korokoro means (1) something round and cute or (2) the chirping of a cricket.

🎧087 グルッと

[gurutto]

円を描くようにひと周りする様子
moving in a circular manner

Example

時間があったので、市街をグルッと1周してみた。
I had some time so I walked around the urban district.

Point ....

Gurutto also describes a circular movement.

Synonym ....

グルリ [gururi]

🎧088 クルクル

[kurukuru]

軽やかに続いて回る様子／ものを何回も回す様子
moving around lightly; spinning something repeatedly

Example

クルクルと美しく回るフィギュアスケーターに見入ってしまう。
When a figure skater spins round and round so beautifully, it is mesmerizing.

Point ···
Kurukuru means a series of circular movements, not a single turn.

Synonym ···
グルグル [guruguru]

Swayng scenes

🎧089 クネクネ
[kunekune]

左右にゆれるように曲がる様子
bending like swaying from
side to side

Example

ハワイアンダンサーの腰が
クネクネと動いている。
The Hawaiian hula dancer is
wiggling her hips.

🎧090 キョロキョロ
[kyorokyoro]

小さく左右に動く様子
swaying sideways a little

Example

キョロキョロと
落ちつきなく周囲を見回す。
He is looking around restlessly
and nervously.

Point ....

Kyorokyoro is used when you
look around.

物の状態を表す

STATE OF THINGS

⌕091 **キラキラ**

[kirakira]

明るくまぶしげに光りかがやく様子
shining brightly and glaringly

Example

夜空を見上げたらたくさんの星が**キラキラ**とかがやいていた。
I looked up at the sky and saw a lot of stars glittering.

Point ···
Kirakira is used to describe light from gemstones, etc.

Note ···
Kirakira also describes as a metaphor for a brilliantly active person.

🎧092 ピカピカ
[pikapika]

真新しくかがやく様子
brand new and shining

ピカピカに磨いた靴は気持ちがいい。
Highly polished shoes feel good.

Note ···

Pikapika is also used to describe brightness when something is blinking or takes a turn.

∩093 ツルツル

[tsurutsuru]

表面が平らで光沢のある様子／物の状態がなめらかな様子

flat, glossy surface; smooth

Example

雪が凍ってツルツルになった道路で転んだ。

I slipped on a slick road that was covered with ice from the melting snow.

Note ⋯⋯⋯⋯⋯⋯⋯⋯⋯⋯⋯⋯⋯⋯⋯⋯⋯⋯⋯⋯⋯⋯⋯⋯⋯⋯⋯⋯⋯⋯

Tsurutsuru also describes how you eat noodles.

🎧094 ぐんぐん

[gungun]

物事が勢いよく進行する様子／成長する様子

things going on vigorously; growth

Example

娘の背丈が最近ぐんぐん伸びてうれしい。

I am happy because my daughter is growing taller and taller steadily.

🎧095 スクスク

[sukusuku]

何もさえぎるものがなく元気に育つ様子／
樹木などが高くまっすぐに伸びる様子

growing in a lively way without obstruction; trees stretching high and straight

Example

気がついたら、夏草がスクスクと伸びていた。

I noticed that the summer grasses grew rapidly.

Note ⋯⋯⋯⋯⋯⋯⋯⋯⋯⋯⋯⋯⋯⋯⋯⋯⋯⋯⋯⋯⋯⋯⋯⋯⋯⋯⋯⋯

Sukusuku also describes child growth.

🎧096 ニョキニョキ
[nyokinyoki]

植物などがあちらこちらに生えてくる様子
plants etc. that are growing here and there

Example

ニョキニョキとたくさんのキノコがはえている。
Many mushrooms are shooting up one after another.

Note ⋯⋯⋯
Nyokinyoki is also used when things appear one after another.

🎧097 くしゃくしゃ

[kushakusha]

紙、布などを音を立てて丸めたりもんで小さくする様子やその音

rolling up or crumpling paper or cloth noisily, especially the sound

Example

書き間違えた手紙を、くしゃくしゃに丸めて捨てた。

I screwed up a letter as I misspelled some words and threw it away.

Note ··

Kushakusha also describes (1) a crying or laughing face or (2) untidy conditions.

∩098 メラメラ

[meramera]

炎を上げて勢いよく燃えたり光ってゆれたりする様子
burning with flames; flickering with light

Example

みんなで焚火をしてメラメラと燃える炎を見つめた。
We made a bonfire and watched the licking flames.

Note ···

Meramera is also used to describe strong emotions like jealousy and anger.

∩099 びちゃびちゃ
[bichabicha]

はげしく水びたしになる様子
severely waterlogged

Example

うっかり深い水たまりに踏み込んで靴が**びちゃびちゃ**になった。
I carelessly stepped into a deep puddle and my shoes became soggy.

Note ....
Bichabicha describes the squelching of water of liquid, especially the sound.

🎧100 ザブザブ

[zabuzabu]

水を大きく動かす様子や、その音

moving water about a lot; especially the sound

Example

夏の朝は、起きて、顔をすぐ水でザブザブと洗うと気持ちがいい。

It is refreshing to wake up and splash my face with water immediately on summer mornings.

🎧101 バシャバシャ

[bashabasha]

水面をたて続けに叩いたり、かき乱したりする様子や、その音

repeatedly hitting or stirring the water's surface; especially the sound

Example

海水浴に行き、水をバシャバシャとかけあった。

We went swimming in the ocean and splashed seawater at each other.

⌕102 すべすべ
[subesube]

手ざわりや見た目がとてもなめらかで快い様子
feeling or looking very smooth and comfortable

Example

赤ちゃんのほっぺたはすべすべしている。
A baby's cheeks are velvety.

🎧103 しっとり
[shittori]

湿り気が全体に行き渡っている様子
completely moist

Example

あのお菓子屋さんのいちおしは、
しっとりしたサバラン※だ。 ※ラム酒漬けケーキ
The cake shop owner recommended the moist savarin.

Note ....
Shittori is also used to describe quiet calmness.

Point ....
Shittori is also used to describe hair or skin.

🎧104 ツヤツヤ

[tsuyatsuya]

光沢があって美しい様子
shiny and beautiful

リップクリームをぬったら、唇がツヤツヤになった。
I put on lip balm and my dry lips became glossy.

Point ....

Tsuyatsuya also describes hair, skin or silk cloth.

🎧105 サラサラ

[sarasara]

好ましい程度に乾いている様子／
つかえがなく、軽くこすれあう様子
agreeably dry; brush against lightly

Example

サラサラのロングヘアーのあの子はみんなのあこがれだ。
She has silky long hair and is everyone's heartthrob.

Note ⋯⋯⋯⋯⋯⋯⋯⋯⋯⋯⋯⋯⋯⋯⋯⋯⋯⋯⋯⋯⋯⋯⋯⋯⋯⋯⋯⋯⋯⋯⋯

Sarasara is also used to describe a delicate sound made when objects lightly touch each other.

🎧106 スラスラ

[surasura]

動作や物事がなめらかで滞りない様子

smooth and without a hitch

Example

何度も挨拶を練習したので、スラスラ言えるようになった。

I practiced the speech again and again so that I could say it smoothly.

🎧107 ドロドロ

[dorodoro]

重たげにとけたり流れたりする様子

melting and flowing heavily

Example

暑い日はソフトクリームがすぐにドロドロに溶けてしまう。

On a hot day, soft-serve ice cream soon melts and gets sticky.

Synonym ···

トロトロ **[torotoro]** smoother than *dorodoro* but still thick

🎧108 ベタベタ

[betabeta]

ものが不快な感じでくっつく様子／必要以上にまとわりつく様子
uncomfortably sticky; clinging unnecessarily

Example

汚れでベタベタしている床をキレイに拭き取る。
I will wipe the dirty, sticky floor.

Note ··

Betabeta also means couples who are clingy in public.

🎧109 カサカサ
[kasakasa]

乾いてうるおいのない様子

dry; not moist

手がカサカサしているので、ハンドクリームが欠かせない。

My hands are rough and dry, so I can't do without hand cream.

Note ···

Kasakasa also means a light sound made when dry, stark objects rub against each other.

∩ 110 パサパサ

[pasapasa]

乾いて水分のない様子や、十分なうるおいがない様子
dry and without fluid; without enough moisture

Example

乾燥して**パサパサ**になったパンはおいしくない。
Dry, mealy bread is not tasty.

Note ⋯⋯⋯
Pasapasa is used to describe damaged hair.

🎧111 ピッタリ

[pittari]

よく合っている様子／すき間なく、くっつきあっている様子
fitting well; touching each other without any gaps

Example

サイズが ピッタリ だったので、その T シャツを買うことにした。
It was perfectly my size so I decided to buy the T shirt.

🎧112 ブカブカ

[bukabuka]

サイズがゆるく、大きすぎる様子
loose and too big in size

Example

お父さんの帽子は私には大きすぎてブカブカだ。
My father's hat is too big and loose-fitting for me.

🎧113 バラバラ

[barabara]

あちこちにある様子や、
ひとつひとつが独立していてまとまりがない様子

being here or there, or each object being independent and
disorganized

Example

みんなの意見がバラバラすぎて、ぜんぜんまとまらない。

Everyone's opinions are so different that we can't come to
an agreement at all.

🎧114 ゴチャゴチャ
[gochagocha]

多様なものが雑然と集まっている様子

different things gathering together untidily

Example

ものがあふれて部屋がゴチャゴチャしていたが
片付けてスッキリした。

The room was full of things and messy so I tidied it up.

Note ···

Gochagocha is also used to describe how you excuse or give a sermon
importunately and untidily.

Disordered scenes

🎧115 **ボサボサ**
[bosabosa]

髪の毛などがみっともなく
乱れている様子

**hair etc. being unattractively
untidy**

Example

寝起きはいつも**ボサボサ**頭だ。
**My hair is always unkempt
when I get up.**

Note ·······································

Bosabosa also describes
absentmindedness or slow movement.

🎧116 **ボロボロ**
[boroboro]

ものがひどく破れたり傷んでいる様子
severely torn or damaged

Example

ボロボロになったけれども思い出のある
ぬいぐるみなので捨てられない。
**The stuffed toy is ragged but I
cannot throw it away because it
has sentimental value.**

Note ·······································

Boroboro also means fragments
spilling down.

物事の程度や様子を表す

DEGREES & MANNERS

もこ もこ

🎧117 ドッサリ

[dossari]

数量がとても多い様子、非常にたくさんある様子
a large quantity; a great number

Example

ドッサリつもった書類を片付けるのが来週までの課題だ。
I have to take care of a pile of documents by next week.

Point ....
Dossari means something abundant and massive.

🎧118 ギュウギュウ

[gyuugyuu]

かたくしめたり、強く押し込んだりする様子
tightening; pushing in hard

Example

朝のラッシュ時の電車の中はいつもギュウギュウに混んでいる。
Rush hour trains are always packed to the gills.

Synonym ···

ギュッと [gyutto] *Gyuugyuu* implies repetitive actions, while *gyutto* is used to describe a single action.

🎧119 ビッシリ

[bisshiri]

すき間がないほど詰め込まれている様子

jammed without any space left

Example

勉強熱心な彼女のノートは、ビッシリと書きこまれている。

She is so hardworking that her notebooks are packed with notes.

⌒120 チョッピリ

[choppiri]

分量や程度のきわめて少ない様子

a very small quantity or degree

Example

瓶に**チョッピリ**残っていたハチミツを味わった。

I tasted a tiny bit of honey that was left in the jar.

🎧121 チビチビ

[chibichibi]

ほんの少しずつ惜しむようにする様子

doing something little by little, almost sparingly

Example

おじいちゃんは、寝る前に チビチビ とウイスキーを飲むのが習慣だ。

My grandfather has a habit of tippling whisky before he goes to bed.

Synonym ....

チョビチョビ [chobichobi] like *chibichibi*, *chobichobi* describes how you deal with a small quantity of something

🎧122 ちょこっと
[chokotto]

程度や時間がほんのわずかな様子
a very small degree or a very short time

Example

帰り際、職員室にちょこっと顔を出した。
I dropped by the teacher's room on my way home.

Synonym ··

ちょっと **[chotto]** compared with *chotto*, *chokotto* emphasizes smallness in amount

🎧123 ほんのり

[honnori]

形、色、香りなどがかすかに現れる様子
some figure, color or scent, etc. appearing faintly

Example

お酒でほんのり色づいた頬がかわいらしい。
Her slightly rosy cheeks after drinking are charming.

∩124 ぼんやり

[bonyari]

色や形がぼやけていてよく見えない様子／
あいまいではっきりしない様子

blurred and hazy colors or shapes; unclear and obscure

Example

ぼんやりと話を聞いていて何も覚えていない。

I was listening to his talk absentmindedly so I don't remember anything.

⌂125 モヤモヤ

[moyamoya]

考えや記憶などがあいまいな様子／
割り切れない感情や気分でいる様子

ambiguous ideas or memories: feeling unconvinced

Example

好きな女の子の本心がつかめなくてモヤモヤとする。

I feel uneasy because I don't understand what my crush really means.

Point ....

Moya, literally light fog, describes how your mind is hazy and vague.

🎧126 あやふや
[ayafuya]

物事が確かでない様子／判断がつかず、決定しない様子

something not being certain; indeterminable and unjudgable

Example

決断を求められて、あやふやな態度をとってしまった。

He hustled me into making a decision, but I could only give him a vague answer.

🎧127 パパッと

[papatto]

手際よくすばやい様子

adept and quick

Example

時間がないときはパパッと片付けることが大切だ。

It is important to get things done swiftly when you have no time.

🎧128 ザッと

[zatto]

動作が急で、ていねいでない様子

rapid movements; not doing something carefully

Example

ザッと見渡したところ、探している書類はここにはないようだ。

I just had a quick look around and I don't think the document I'm looking for is here.

🎧129 グズグズ

[guzuguzu]

行動や動作の手際が悪く、無駄に時間がかかる様子／
進み方がとどこおっている様子

expeditious actions or movements causing unnecessary
time loss; stagnating

Example

もう出かける時間なのにまだグズグズしている。

It's time to leave, but he is still dawdling.

Point

Guzuguzu is also used to describe a stuffy nose.

🎧130 モタモタ

[motamota]

行動や態度の決定がにぶく遅い様子
slow to act or make a decision

改札口でモタモタしていたら、電車に乗り遅れてしまった。
I dilly-dallied at the ticket gate and missed the train.

🎧131 のろのろ
[noronoro]

動きがにぶく遅い様子
slow-moving

のろのろと走っていたら、どんどんぬかされてしまった。
I drove slowly and everyone passed me.

🎧132 のんびり
[nonbiri]

何にとらわれるでもなく、心身ともにくつろいでいる様子
not bound by anything and relaxed both physically and mentally

Example

南の島でのんびり過ごして羽をのばしたい。
I'd like to relax and have a great time on a tropical island.

🎧133 まったり
[mattari]

無駄な力が入らず、落ちついてくつろいでいる様子
relaxed, calm and comfortable

Example

友人とお茶をしながら**まったり**する時間は大切だ。
Time to chill out and drink tea with my friends is precious to me.

Note ··

Mattari also describes (1) a rich flavor or (2) slow movement or progress.

🎧134 カチコチ

[kachikochi]

物がとても固くなっている様子

something getting very hard

Example

冬の朝、バケツの水が凍って、表面がカチコチに固まっていた。

It was a winter morning and the surface of the water in a bucket was frozen solid.

Note ···

Kachikochi also means (1) a sound made when a hard object hits something or (2) stiff body movement due to stress.

∩135 ふにゃふにゃ
[funyafunya]

やわらかくて張りがなく弱々しい様子
soft, loose and feeble

Example

段ボールが水に濡れて**ふにゃふにゃ**になってしまった。
The cardboard got wet and flabby.

🎧136 ふわふわ
[fuwafuwa]

やわらかくふくらんでいる様子
soft and swelled

このパンケーキはふわふわしていておいしい。
This pancake is fluffy and tasty.

Note ···

Fuwafuwa is also used to describe (1) drifting around or (2) volatile, unsettled mind and movement.

Soft scenes

🎧137 フカフカ
[fukafuka]

やわらかく適度な弾力で
ふくらんでいる様子

**softly swelling with
adequate elasticity**

Example

フカフカのクッションが
お気に入りだ。

I love fluffy cushions.

🎧138 モコモコ
[mokomoko]

やわらかくふくらんで
厚みがある様子

soft, swelling and thick

Example

羊の毛はモコモコしていて
あたたかそうだ。

**Sheep wool is lumpy and
looks warm.**

温度や天気の いろいろ

TEMPERATURES & WEATHER

🎧139 ポカポカ

[pokapoka]

おだやかであたたかな様子

calm and warm

Example

今日はポカポカとあたたかい、いいお天気だ。

It is a pleasant, balmy day.

Note ···

Pokapoka also describes tapping sounds.

🎧140 ぬくぬく

[nukunuku]

気持ちよくあたたかいものの中に身をおく様子
staying in something comfortable and warm

Example

この毛布はぬくぬくしていて気持ちがいい。
This blanket is snug and comfy.

Note ··

Nukunuku is also used when you alone live on easy street without making any effort.

🎧141 ムシムシ

[mushimushi]

暑くて湿気が多い様子
hot and humid

Example

ムシムシしていて寝にくい夜だ。
It's muggy and hard to sleep tonight.

🎧142 ジリジリ

[jirijiri]

太陽がやけつくように強く照りつける様子

scorching hot sun

Example

ジリジリとした暑さが続いていて夏バテしそうだ。

It's been sizzlingly hot and the summer heat is almost killing me.

🎧143 ゾクゾク

[zokuzoku]

寒さや恐れなどで唇や体が奥底から小刻みにふるえる様子

your lips or body trembling strongly due to cold or fear

昨夜はゾクゾクするくらいの寒さだった。

It was freezing cold last night.

🎧144 ヒンヤリ

[hinyari]

体の表面に冷たさを感じる様子

feeling cold on the surface of a body

Example

昼間は暖かかったが、夜になるとヒンヤリとしてきた。

It was warm during the daytime, but I began to feel chilly at night.

Point ··

Hinyari is often used to describe the temperature of food and beverages as well as air temperature.

⌂145 どんより

[donyori]

空が重く曇って薄暗い様子
cloudy, gloomy sky

Example

どんよりとした空で今にも雨が降りそうだ。
It's overcast and looks like it's going to rain at any moment.

Point ···
Donyori means sombre atmosphere under grey skies.

Note ···
Donyori also means gloom as if a dark cloud is hovering over your heart.

🎧146 ジメジメ

[jimejime]

ひどく湿気を帯びて、不快、不潔、陰気な感じのする様子
very humid, feeling uncomfortable, filthy and overcast

Example

このところ雨が降り続いて、ジメジメする。
It's raining and damp these days.

🎧147 しとしと

[shitoshito]

雨などが、こまやかで静かに降る様子
drizzling rain, etc. falling quietly

Example

しとしとと降る雨の中を歩いてすっかり濡れてしまった。
I got soaked when I was walking in the drizzling rain.

Point ⋯⋯⋯⋯⋯⋯⋯⋯⋯⋯⋯⋯⋯⋯⋯⋯⋯⋯⋯⋯⋯⋯⋯⋯⋯⋯⋯⋯⋯⋯⋯
Shitoshito describes a long spell of rain.

Rain scenes

🎧148 ポツポツ
[potsupotsu]

雨などが、小さな粒で降り始める様子
a sprinkle of rain, etc. beginning to fall

Example

朝から曇り空だったが、
ポツポツと雨が降り始めた。

It had been gray and overcast
since this morning and it began
to sprinkle a little bit.

Note ·····································

Potsupotsu also means (1) a lot of round
protrusions or holes or (2) interspersion.

🎧149 ザーザー
[zaazaa]

雨がはげしく降る音や、その様子
raining hard, especially the
sound

Example

出かけたいのに、
ザーザーと雨が降って止まない。

I want to go out, but the rain is
pouring down and not stopping.

Wind scenes

🎧150 そよそよ
[soyosoyo]

風がゆっくり静かに吹く様子
wind blowing gently and slowly

Example

そよそよと吹く春風が気持ちいい。
A nice, soft breeze is blowing.

🎧151 ビュービュー
[byuubyuu]

強い風が鋭く吹く音や、その様子
a strong wind blowing hard,
especially the sound

Example

ビュービュー吹く風に
洗濯物があおられる。
The wuthering wind is flapping
the laundry.

Synonym ·······································

ヒューヒュー [hyuuhyuu] wind weaker than byuubyuu.
Hyuuhyuu is also an shout of ridicule.

食事や料理に使う表現

FOOD & CUISINE

キンキン

🎧152 パクパク

[pakupaku]

ものを軽やかに盛んに食べる様子

eating lightly and vigorously

Example

みんなでパクパク食べていたら
あっという間にクッキーがなくなった。

Everyone munched the cookies and they disappeared
instantly.

Synonym ....

パクリ [pakuri] *Pakupaku* means continuous movement while pakuri means a
huge bite.

🎧153 モグモグ

[mogumogu]

物を口にほおばり、口を開けずに何度もかむ様子

filling your mouth and chewing food repeatedly without opening your mouth

Example

子どもが口いっぱいにお菓子を入れてモグモグしている。

Children are mumbling with their mouths full of snacks.

♫154 ガツガツ
[gatsugatsu]

非常に勢いよくむさぼり食う様子
fiercely devouring a meal

Example

とてもお腹がすいていたので、ガツガツ食べてしまった。
I was so hungry that I ate ravenously.

Synonym

ガッツリ [gattsuri] Gatsugatsu describes vigorous devour, though gattsuri means eating a lot of enough food.

🎧155 ペロペロ

[peropero]

物を舌の先で何度もなめあげる様子

running the tip of your tongue over something again and again

Example

子どもがソフトクリームをペロペロとなめている。

A child is licking soft serve with her tongue.

🎧156 ガブガブ

[gabugabu]

飲み物を非常に勢いよく大量に飲む様子や、その音
drinking a lot of liquid vigorously, especially the sound

Example

とても喉がかわいていたので、水を ガブガブ 飲んでしまった。
I was really thirsty and took a swig of water.

🎧157 グビグビ

[gubigubi]

おいしそうに息もつかずに飲み物を飲む様子や、その音

drinking a beverage with relish without even taking a breath, especially the sound

Example

お父さんは久しぶりのビールをうれしそうにグビグビ飲んでいる。

My father is joyfully chugging his first beer in a long time.

Point ···

Gubigubi often describes drinking alcohol.

🎧158 ゴクゴク

[gokugoku]

のどを鳴らしながら一気に飲む様子や、その音

gulping down quickly, especially the sound

Example

お風呂上りにアイスカフェオレをゴクゴク飲んだ。

I gulped down iced coffee with milk after taking a bath.

Synonym ....

ゴクリ [gokuri] *Gokugoku* means continuous gulping while *gokuri* describes one big gulp.

🎧159 チューチュー

[chuuchuu]

口を細めて飲み物を少しずつ吸う様子や、その音

puckering your lips and sucking a drink little by little, especially the sound

Example

ジュースをストローでチューチューと飲んだ。

I sucked juice through a straw.

Note ⋯⋯⋯⋯⋯⋯⋯⋯⋯⋯⋯⋯⋯⋯⋯⋯⋯⋯⋯⋯⋯⋯⋯⋯⋯⋯⋯⋯⋯⋯

Chuchu is also used to describe the squeaks of a mouse.

🎧160 アッサリ

[assari]

人や物事の状態・性質が、淡泊である様子

someone or something being straightforward and plain

Example

ちょっと胃が重いので**アッサリ**としたものが食べたい。

I have a bloated stomach and want to eat a plain meal.

Note ···

Assari also means a straightforward and laidback person.

🎧161 コッテリ

[kotteri]

しつこいぐらい濃厚な様子
persistently thick and rich

Example

彼はコッテリした味のラーメンに目がない。
He has a weakness for rich ramen.

🎧162 ジュージュー

[jyuujyuu]

魚や肉などを強火で焼くときに出る音や、その様子

frying fish or meat with a high flame, especially the sound

Example

フライパンからジュージューとハンバーグの焼ける音がする。

I can hear the sizzling sounds of the hamburger steak in the frying pan.

Point ....

Jyujyu typically describes the sizzling sound made when you cook with a frying pan.

🎧163 こんがり

[kongari]

ちょうどよい焼き色がついて、香ばしく焼ける様子
adequately browned and nice-smelling

Example

こんがり焼けたおいしいトーストを朝食に食べた。
I ate some tasty brown toast for breakfast.

Note ⋯⋯⋯⋯⋯⋯⋯⋯⋯⋯⋯⋯⋯⋯⋯⋯⋯⋯⋯⋯⋯⋯⋯⋯⋯⋯⋯⋯⋯⋯
Kongari also means suntanned skin.

🎧164 グツグツ

[gutsugutsu]

グツグツ

強い火力で煮込むときの音や、その様子
boiling at a high heat, especially the sound

Example

寒い日には、グツグツと煮込んだ鍋が食べたい。
I like to eat simmered nabe on a cold day.

Point ··
Gutsugutsu is often used to describe the sound of cooking with a pot.

🎧165 コトコト

[kotokoto]

鍋の中のものが弱火で静かに煮える音や、その様子

something in a pot being cooked slowly and quietly, especially the sound

Example

コトコトと煮込んだスープをいただく。

I really like a stew that has been slowly cooked for hours.

🎧166 ホカホカ

[hokahoka]

心地よいあたたかさを感じたり、適度にあたたかい様子

feeling comfortably warm; adequately warm

ホカホカのごはんに焼肉をのせて食べる。

I'll eat rice straight from the cooker after topping it with roast meat.

🎧167 キンキン

[kinkin]

とても冷たく、強く張りつめていたり、
その感覚を生じたりするような様子

very cold; very tense, or making someone feel so

Example

うだるような暑さのなか帰宅して真っ先に
キンキンに冷えたビールを飲む。

On a sweltering hot day, I come home and drink ice-cold beer first.

Point ··

Kinkin is often used to describe ice-cold beer.

🎧168 サクサク

[sakusaku]

物をかむときなどの連続する心地よい印象の音やその様子

doing some action (for example, biting something) repeatedly and giving an agreeable impression, especially the sound

Example

サクサクのクッキーが焼けたので、友人にプレゼントした。

I baked crisp cookies and gave them to a friend.

Note ⋯⋯⋯⋯⋯⋯⋯⋯⋯⋯⋯⋯⋯⋯⋯⋯⋯⋯⋯⋯⋯⋯⋯⋯⋯⋯⋯⋯⋯⋯⋯⋯⋯⋯

Sakusaku also means things going on smoothly (see p. 33).

🎧169 トロリ
[torori]

とけてやわらかくなる様子
melted and softened

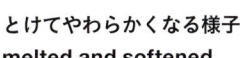

ピザの上のトロリととろけるチーズが食欲をそそる。
A pizza oozing with cheese is so appetizing.

Point ···

Torori can emphasize stretch.

Texture 1

🎧170 シャキシャキ
[shakishaki]

水気の多い野菜などを歯切れよく
噛む音や、その様子

**the sound of biting fresh
vegetables crisply**

Example

新鮮で**シャキシャキ**の
レタスが入った
サンドイッチを作った。

**I made sandwiches with
fresh, crunchy lettuce.**

🎧171 トロトロ
[torotoro]

柔らかく流れ出しそうな様子／とろみのある液体

soft, flowing out; thick liquid

Example

トロトロ卵のオムライスは
この店の看板メニューだ。

**Soufflé omelette with rice
is the signature dish of this
restaurant.**

Note ⋯⋯⋯⋯⋯⋯⋯⋯⋯⋯⋯⋯⋯⋯⋯

Torotoro describes (1) a slow,
inefficient person or (2) a low fire.

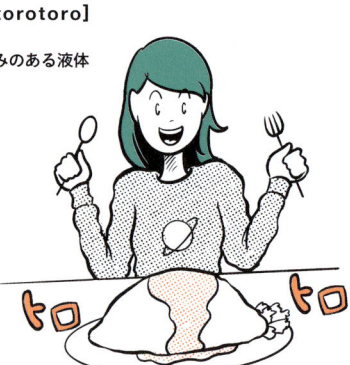

Texture 2

🎧172 ネバネバ
[nebaneba]

糸をひくような粘着性がある様子
stringy and sticky

Example

オクラや納豆などの
ネバネバ食材は体にいい。
Gooey foods like okra and natto are good for your health.

🎧173 プルプル
[purupuru]

弾力があって小きざみに
揺れ動く様子や、食感
elastic and wobbly

Example

よく冷やしたプルプルのゼリーは
夏のおやつに最適だ。
Well-chilled jiggly jelly is a perfect summer dessert.

Texture 3

🎧174 モチモチ
[mochimochi]

心地よくほどよい粘り気と
弾力が感じられる様子

**feeling comfortably sticky and
elastic**

Example

モチモチとした
パンがお気に入りだ。

**My favorite food is chewy
bread.**

🎧175 ホクホク
[hokuhoku]

水けやねばりけなどが少なく、口の中でやわらかくほぐれ崩れる様子

**not juicy or sticky, loosening
softly in your mouth**

Example

茹でてホクホクのじゃがいもに
バターをのせるとおいしい。

**Soft and flaky boiled potatoes
topped with butter are tasty.**

Point ··

Hokuhoku is often used to describe starchy
food like roast potatoes and squash.

音のいろいろ

SOUNDS

リン

リン

🎧176 コンコン

[konkon]

固いものが打ち当たってたてる軽く明るい音

a light, clear sound made when something solid hits a hard surface

ドアを開ける前に、コンコンとノックする。

I knocked on the door before opening it.

Note ....

Konkon is also used to describe coughing and its sound.

🎧177 ポンポン

[ponpon]

物を軽くたたく音やその様子／
また、物が破裂するときの高い音

patting something, especially the sound; plosive sound

Example

ポンポンと肩をたたかれてはっと振り向いたら先生だった。

Someone patted my shoulder; I turned around and found it was my teacher.

Synonym ···

ポン [pon] *Ponpon* describes continuous patting, while *pon* means one light pat.

∩178 パチパチ
[pachipachi]

続けざまにひびく、するどく小さい音
sharp, small repeated sounds

Example

パチパチと思わず手をたたいてしまうくらいよい歌だった。
The song was so good that I unconsciously clapped my hands.

Note ···
Pachipachi describes a roaring fire or its sound.

🎧179 バンバン

[banban]

ものを強く力任せにたたいたり置いたりするときや、
破裂するときの重みのある音

loud sounds made when you hit a hard surface or put
something down with brute force or burst something

Example

机を両手でバンバンと叩いて怒りをあらわにする。

I bang the table with my palms to express anger.

Synonym ··

バン **[ban]** *Banban* describes continuous movements, while ban means one light
pat.

🎧180 ガサゴソ

[gasagoso]

薄く張りのあるもの同士が強く触れ合って発する、やや騒がしい音

a rather loud sound made when thin and tense objects bang against each other

Example

かばんの中を探してガサゴソと音をたてる。

I make a rustling noise when I search my bag for something.

🎧181 ゴシゴシ

[goshigoshi]

強く力を入れて、ものを何度もこする際の音やその様子

rubbing something repeatedly with power, especially the sound

Example

台所のシンクの頑固な汚れをゴシゴシと磨いて落とす。

I scrub the kitchen sink to remove the tough stains.

⌒182 ゴリゴリ

[gorigori]

強く力を込めてこすったり、踏みつけたり、
かんだりする音やその様子

**strongly rubbing, stamping or chewing something,
especially the sound**

Example

ごまをすり鉢で**ゴリゴリ**とすって風味を出す。

I grind sesame seeds hard in a mortar to draw out the
flavor.

Note ⋯⋯⋯⋯⋯⋯⋯⋯⋯⋯⋯⋯⋯⋯⋯⋯⋯⋯⋯⋯⋯⋯⋯⋯⋯⋯⋯⋯⋯⋯⋯⋯⋯⋯⋯⋯

Gorigori is also used to describe how someone pushes ahead.

⌂183 ジャラジャラ

[jyarajyara]

小石、硬貨などの小さくかたいものがたくさんふれ合ってたてる音
a sound made when small, hard objects like small stones
or coins come in contact with each other

Example

ポケットに入れた小銭がジャラジャラと音をたてる。
The coins in my pocket are making jangling sounds.

🎧184 コツン

[kotsun]

かたいものを一度打ち当てたとき、
ぶつかってたてる軽く高い音やその様子

a hard object bumping once, especially a light, high sound

Example

風で飛んだ木の実が窓にあたってコツンという音がした。

A nut from the tree hit the window and made a clicking sound.

🎧185 ガシャン

[gashan]

かたいもの同士がぶつかり合うときに出る重く強い音

a heavy, strong sound made when hard objects hit each other

列車の車両が ガシャン という音をたてて連結した。

The train cars made a loud clashing sound and connected to each other.

Note ⋯⋯⋯⋯⋯⋯⋯⋯⋯⋯⋯⋯⋯⋯⋯⋯⋯⋯⋯⋯⋯⋯⋯⋯⋯⋯⋯⋯⋯⋯⋯⋯

Gashan is also used to describe how glass breaks.

⌒186 チャリンチャリン

［charincharin］

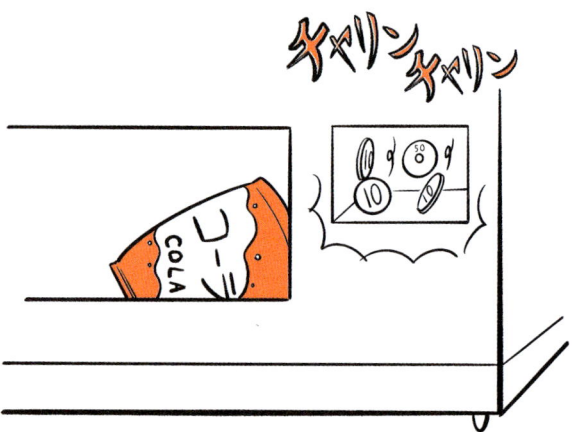

軽い金属同士が何度か触れ合ったり
ぶつかったりしてたてる高くひびく音

high-pitched ringing sounds made when light metal objects
hit or touch each other several times

Example

チャリンチャリンと自動販売機からお釣りが出てきた。

The vending machine clinked and gave back change.

Synonym ....

チャリン [charin] You don't always have to say charin twice.

🎧187 ピーポーピーポー

[piipoopiipoo]

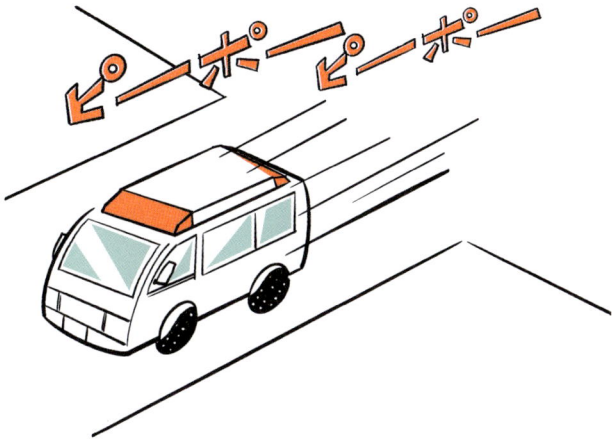

救急車のサイレンなどに用いられる高くするどい電子音

electronic sound that is high and sharp; such as the siren of an ambulance

Example

救急車が交差点をピーポーピーポーという音とともに過ぎ去った。

An ambulance with its siren on passed through the intersection.

🎧188 ウーウー

[wuuwuu]

パトカーや消防車などのサイレンの音
siren of police cars or fire engines

Example

消防車がウーウーというサイレンの音を鳴らしながら現場に向かう。
A fire engine with its siren on rushes to the scene.

Note ⋯⋯⋯⋯⋯⋯⋯⋯⋯⋯⋯⋯⋯⋯⋯⋯⋯⋯⋯⋯⋯⋯⋯⋯⋯⋯⋯⋯⋯⋯⋯⋯⋯
Wuuwuu also describes a roar or growl.

⌂189 ドーン

[doon]

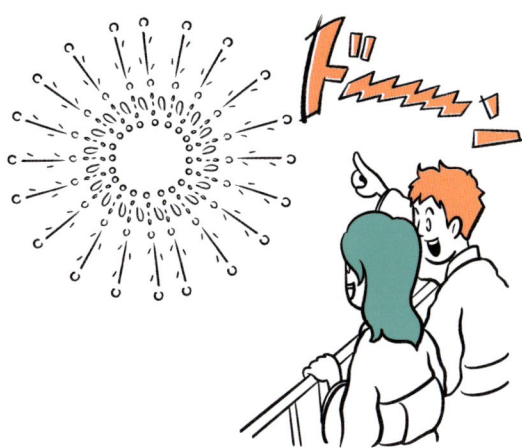

火薬が爆発するときの大きな音や、
人や物が勢いよくぶつかる音やその様子

gunpowder being exploded, or someone/something hitting hard, especially the sound

Example

夏の夜空に花火があがり、そのあと少したって、ドーンと響く音がした。

Fireworks exploded in the summer night sky and boomed after a short while.

Note ....

Doon also describes the sound of a drum.

Instruments 1

🎧190 ドンドコ
[dondoko]

太鼓を勢いよく叩くときなどの重くにぶくひびく音やその様子

someone beating a drum forcefully, especially a deep sound

Example

お祭り会場のある遠くのほうから
ドンドコという音が聞こえてくる。

The rolling sound of drums traveled far from the festival venue.

Point ....

Dondoko implies bustle.

🎧191 リンリン
[rinrin]

鈴やベルなどの金属が勢いよく触れ合って鳴る音

the sound of a bell; the sound made when metal objects touch each other vigorously

Example

子どもがリンリンと
鈴を鳴らしている。

A child is tinkling a bell.

Point ....

Rinrin also describes the sound of singing crickets (suzumushi).

Instruments 2

🎧192 ピーヒャラ
[piihyara]

笛などの高く鳴りひびく音
a high, resonant sound of a flute, etc.

Example

ピーヒャラと楽しそうな
笛の音が聞こえる。

I can hear the light, cheerful
notes of a flute.

Point ··································

Piihyara is mainly used to refer to the
sound of a flute.

🎧193 シャカシャカ
[shakashaka]

マラカスやタンバリンを
ふったときなどの軽く硬質な音
a light, solid sound of the
maracas or tambourine

Example

リズミカルにシャカシャカと
マラカスをふった。

I played the maracas
rhythmically and briskly.

🎧194 ワンワン

[wanwan]

イヌの鳴き声／また、イヌをあらわす幼児語
a dog bark; also baby talk for dog

Example

お隣のイヌがワンワンと元気よく鳴いている。
Our neighbor's dog is bow-wowing excitedly.

Note ⋯⋯⋯⋯⋯⋯⋯⋯⋯⋯⋯⋯⋯⋯⋯⋯⋯⋯⋯⋯⋯⋯⋯⋯⋯⋯⋯⋯⋯⋯

Wanwan is also used to describe intense crying.

🎧195 ニャーニャー

[nyaanyaa]

ネコの鳴き声
a cat's meow

Example

そのネコは目が合うとニャーニャーと鳴いた。
The cat meowed when she caught my eye.

Animal 1

🎧**196 モー**

[moo]

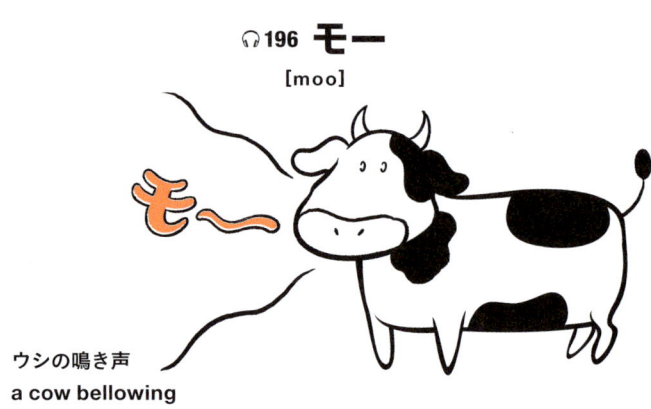

ウシの鳴き声
a cow bellowing

🎧**197 メー**

[mee]

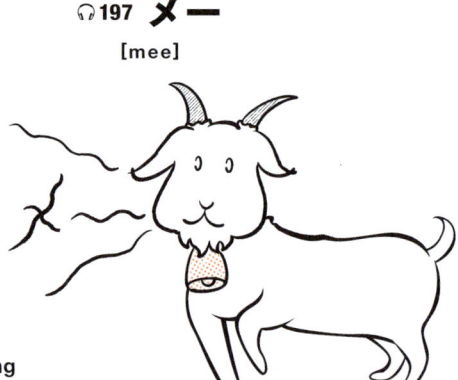

ヤギの鳴き声
a sheep bleating

Animal 2

🎧198 **チュンチュン**
[chunchun]

小鳥のさえずり
a bird chirping

🎧199 **コケコッコー**
[kokekokkoo]

ニワトリの鳴き声
a rooster crowing

Animal 3

🎧200 ヒヒーン
[hihiin]

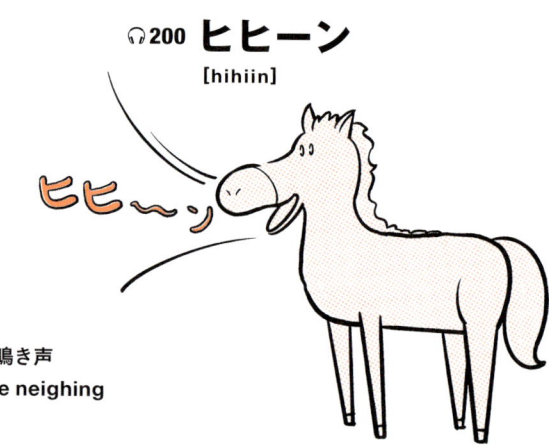

ウマの鳴き声
a horse neighing

🎧201 パオーン
[paoon]

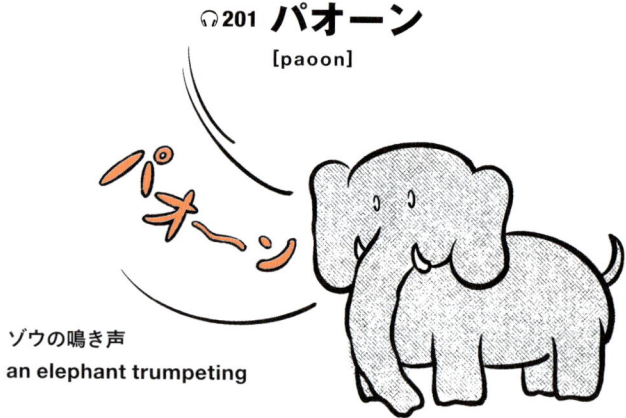

ゾウの鳴き声
an elephant trumpeting

INDEX

索引

A

assari アッサリ ››› 166
atafuta アタフタ ››› 42
ayafuya あやふや ››› 133

B

bakitto バキッと ››› 91
banban バンバン ››› 183
barabara バラバラ ››› 120
bashabasha バシャバシャ ››› 108
betabeta ベタベタ ››› 115
bichabicha びちゃびちゃ ››› 106
bikutto ビクッと ››› 52
bisshiri ビッシリ ››› 126
bonyari ぼんやり ››› 131
boroboro ボロボロ ››› 122
bosabosa ボサボサ ››› 122
bukabuka ブカブカ ››› 119
buruburu ぶるぶる ››› 36
butsubutsu ぶつぶつ ››› 27
byuubyuu ビュービュー ››› 156

C

chakkari ちゃっかり ››› 74
charincharin チャリンチャリン ››› 190
chibichibi チビチビ ››› 128
chikuchiku チクチク ››› 67
chirachira ちらちら ››› 30
chokichoki チョキチョキ ››› 35
chokotto ちょこっと ››› 129
choppiri チョッピリ ››› 127
chunchun チュンチュン ››› 199
chuuchuu チューチュー ››› 165

D

daradara ダラダラ ››› 63
dokidoki ドキドキ ››› 49
dondoko ドンドコ ››› 194
donyori どんより ››› 152
doon ドーン ››› 193
dorodoro ドロドロ ››› 114
dosatto ドサッと ››› 88
dossari ドッサリ ››› 124

E

een エーン ››› 13

F

fukafuka フカフカ ››› 144

funyafunya ふにゃふにゃ ››› 142

furafura フラフラ ››› 84

fuwafuwa ふわふわ ››› 143

G

gaan ガーン ››› 55

gabatto ガバッと ››› 38

gabugabu ガブガブ ››› 162

gakkari がっかり ››› 54

gakugaku ガクガク ››› 37

garigari ガリガリ ››› 76

gasagoso ガサゴソ ››› 184

gashan ガシャン ››› 189

gasshiri ガッシリ ››› 78

gatagata ガタガタ ››› 85

gatsugatsu ガツガツ ››› 160

gayagaya がやがや ››› 34

geragera ゲラゲラ ››› 9

gikutto ギクッと ››› 53

gochagocha ゴチャゴチャ ››› 121

gokugoku ゴクゴク ››› 164

gorigori ゴリゴリ ››› 186

goshigoshi ゴシゴシ ››› 185

gubigubi グビグビ ››› 163

gungun ぐんぐん ››› 101

guragura グラグラ ››› 83

gurutto グルッと ››› 94

gussuri ぐっすり ››› 39

gutsugutsu グツグツ ››› 170

guttari ぐったり ››› 65

guuguu グーグー 40

guzuguzu グズグズ ››› 136

gyuugyuu ギュウギュウ ››› 125

H

hakihaki ハキハキ ››› 28

hakkiri ハッキリ ››› 75

harahara ハラハラ ››› 47

hetoheto ヘトヘト ››› 64

hihiin ヒヒーン ››› 200

hinyari ヒンヤリ ››› 151

hirahira ひらひら ››› 86

hisohiso ひそひそ ››› 29

hokahoka ホカホカ ››› 172

hokuhoku ほくほく ››› 19

hokuhoku ホクホク ››› 178

honnori ほんのり ››› 130

horori ホロリ ››› 51

hyorohyoro ヒョロヒョロ ››› 77

J

jiin ジーン ››› 50

jimejime ジメジメ ››› 153

jinjin ジンジン ››› 68

jirijiri ジリジリ ››› 149

jirojiro ジロジロ ››› 31

jitabata ジタバタ ››› 45

jyarajyara ジャラジャラ ››› 187

jyuujyuu ジュージュー ››› 168

K

kachikochi カチコチ ››› 141

kankan カンカン ››› 17

karakara カラカラ ››› 57

kasakasa カサカサ ››› 116

kicchiri キッチリ ››› 71

kinkin キンキン ››› 173

kirakira キラキラ ››› 98

kokekokkoo コケコッコー
››› 199

kongari こんがり ››› 169

konkon コンコン ››› 180

korokoro コロコロ ››› 93

kotokoto コトコト ››› 171

kotsun コツン ››› 188

kotteri コッテリ ››› 167

kunekune クネクネ ››› 96

kurukuru クルクル ››› 95

kushakusha くしゃくしゃ
››› 104

kusukusu クスクス ››› 11

kyorokyoro キョロキョロ
››› 96

kyun キュン ››› 61

M

mattari まったり ››› 140

mee メー ››› 198

meramera メラメラ ››› 105

mochimochi モチモチ ››› 178

mogumogu モグモグ ››› 159

mojimoji もじもじ ››› 59

mokomoko モコモコ ›››144

moo モー ›››198

motamota モタモタ ›››137

moyamoya モヤモヤ ›››132

muchimuchi ムチムチ ›››80

mukamuka ムカムカ ›››16

mushimushi ムシムシ ›››148

muzumuzu ムズムズ ›››66

N

nebaneba ネバネバ ›››177

nikoniko ニコニコ ›››8

niyaniya ニヤニヤ ›››10

nonbiri のんびり ›››139

noronoro のろのろ ›››138

nukunuku ぬくぬく ›››147

nyaanyaa ニャーニャー ›››197

nyokinyoki ニョキニョキ ›››103

O

orooro オロオロ ›››44

ottori おっとり ›››72

P

pachipachi パチパチ ›››182

pakupaku パクパク ›››158

paoon パオーン ›››200

papatto パパッと ›››134

parapara パラパラ ›››89

pasapasa パサパサ ›››117

pekopeko ペコペコ ›››56

perapera ペラペラ ›››26

peropero ペロペロ ›››161

piihyara ピーヒャラ ›››195

piipoopiipoo ピーポーピーポー ›››191

pikapika ピカピカ ›››99

pittari ピッタリ ›››118

pocchari ぽっちゃり ›››79

pochan ポチャン ›››87

pokapoka ポカポカ ›››146

pokin ポキン ›››90

ponpon ポンポン ›››181

potsupotsu ポツポツ ›››155

pukapuka プカプカ ›››92

pukupuku プクプク ›››80

punpun プンプン ›››15

purupuru プルプル ›› 177

pyonpyon ぴょんぴょん ›› 25

R

ranran ランラン ›› 20

rinrin リンリン ›› 194

runrun ルンルン ›› 20

S

sabasaba サバサバ ›› 73

sakusaku サクサク ›› 33

sakusaku サクサク ›› 174

sappari サッパリ ›› 70

sarasara サラサラ ›› 112

sekaseka せかせか ›› 43

shakashaka シャカシャカ ›› 195

shakishaki シャキシャキ ›› 176

shikushiku しくしく ›› 12

shitoshito しとしと ›› 154

shittori しっとり ›› 110

sowasowa ソワソワ ›› 46

soyosoyo そよそよ ›› 156

subesube すべすべ ›› 109

sukusuku スクスク ›› 102

surasura スラスラ ›› 113

sutasuta スタスタ ›› 22

T

tekipaki テキパキ ›› 32

tekuteku てくてく ›› 24

torori トロリ ›› 175

torotoro トロトロ ›› 176

tsurutsuru ツルツル ›› 100

tsuyatsuya ツヤツヤ ›› 111

U

ujiuji うじうじ ›› 58

ukiuki ウキウキ ›› 18

unzari ウンザリ ›› 62

urouro ウロウロ ›› 23

utouto ウトウト ›› 40

uttori うっとり ›› 60

W

wakuwaku ワクワク ›› 48

wanwan わんわん ›› 14

wanwan ワンワン ›› 196

wuuwuu ウーウー ›› 192

 Y

yurayura ユラユラ ›››　82

Z

zaazaa ザーザー ›››　155

zabuzabu ザブザブ ›››　107

zatto ザッと ›››　135

zokuzoku ゾクゾク ›››　150

zukizuki ズキズキ ›››　68

監修者　小野正弘（Ono Masahiro）
1958 年、岩手県生まれ。明治大学文学部教授。日本語学会副会長・日本近代語研究会会長。専門は日本語の史的研究（文字・語彙・意味）。日本語およびオノマトペに関する著書多数。

ブックデザイン	内藤悠二
イラスト	岡村亮太
英文執筆	小野寺粛
英文チェック	久松紀子
英文校正	フレヤ・マーティン
編集協力	吉原朋江（株式会社スリーシーズン）
編集担当	小髙真梨（ナツメ出版企画株式会社）

ONOMATOPE
The Fantastic World of Japanese Symbolic Words

ナツメ社Webサイト
https://www.natsume.co.jp
書籍の最新情報（正誤情報を含む）は
ナツメ社Webサイトをご覧ください。

2019 年 12 月 5 日　初版発行

監修者	小野正弘	Ono Masahiro, 2019
発行者	田村正隆	

発行所　株式会社ナツメ社
　　　　〒 101-0051 東京都千代田区神田神保町 1-52 ナツメ社ビル 1F
　　　　TEL 03-3291-1257（代表）　FAX 03-3291-5761
　　　　振替 00130-1-58661
制　作　ナツメ出版企画株式会社
　　　　〒 101-0051 東京都千代田区神田神保町 1-52 ナツメ社ビル 3F
　　　　TEL 03-3295-3921（代表）
印刷所　ラン印刷社

ISBN978- 4-8163-6734-2　　　　　　　　　　　　Printed in Japan